The Road to Damascus

This book is dedicated to Lisi Cuckler & Derek Lankford

Special thanks to Pastor Al Cooper having you as my pastor has changed my life forever.

Chapter 1

The Beginning

I must start this book giving all honor and glory to my savior Jesus Christ. Without Him this story would have never been told. I was born April 26, 1990, in Columbus OH, and spent most of my life on the Northside of Columbus. I do not remember a lot of my childhood growing up, just bits and pieces of faded memories. It was not all bad, most of it was spent with my Nana Carmen Higgins who was a loving Grandma. She was one of those people who truly demonstrated unconditional love to me. No matter how much wrong I did she always believed in me and was always there.

My Nana was born in West Virginia and her mother's name was Edna Cassis. We are called Edna Siti which means great grandma in Syrian. They were a religious group of people who went to church every Sunday and a lot different from the environment I grew accustomed to. Nana was a very emotional person unlike her daughter.

The woman that God used to bring me into this world is Tina Lee Higgins. Some have said she resembles Cher. She has long black hair, high cheekbones, from the Cherokee blood running through our veins. My Mother was and still is one of the most determined people I know. When she sets her mind to something she does it no matter the obstacle. I remember the time I was sitting in her car. I must have been about 8 years old, and my mom said, "Kirk picture a rose in your mind". She said, "Can you see it?" "Can you smell it?" "Can you feel it?' I told her "Yes Mom" she said, "Then who's to say it isn't real?"

As I look back on this memory, I see what my mom was teaching me. That even though you cannot experience something with your five senses does not mean it is not real. I will never forget this moment and when I came into the Kingdom of God it prepared me for the truth about real faith the bible speaks about in Hebrews 11:1 "Now faith is the substance of things hoped for, the evidence of things not seen" and this kind of faith only comes by the avenue of hearing and hearing by the word of God.

My earthly Father was not really around. Our relationship consisted of empty promises over telephone conversations filled with past regrets. My Dad left my mother when I was a baby and honestly, I did not blame him.

It was hard for my mother raising two kids on her own. We did not always have the nicest things, but we were always provided for. She was really big on controlling every aspect of our lives.

Before I go too far, I must say that I do not fault my mom for anything I went through as a child. I love my mother and honor her as the word teaches. Today she is a born-again believer and loves the Lord. I truly believe she did the best with what she had to give. I learned to experience life to the overflow John 10:10 what Jesus Christ came to bring every born-again tongue speaking believer you must walk in love. With God's grace I am able to walk in that love and not hold grudges today.

Growing up in my house I always looked at it as the house of horrors. I once told my mom that no matter how much light she let in it could not change the darkness. The bible says where envy and strife is there is confusion and every evil work James 3:16 so growing up I could feel those spirits of darkness.

As a man of God today I wage war with Satan and his camp. I can recognize him so easily because I grew up with his demons in my home. Jesus once told me, "To know thy God is to know thy enemy, to know thy enemy is to know thy God". Meaning if you do not know the Characteristics of your enemy then you can be deceived and will end up choosing the wrong God and fighting the wrong fight.

In John 8:44 Jesus was speaking to the religious group the Pharisees who were all about keeping the Law and teaching the law. This is what religion teaches us: a series of laws that is impossible for you to fulfill. Its design was to reveal to man his nature and draw man back to God. The law showed you your sin, but it never gave you power over it. In Matthew 5:17-20 Jesus taught that He was the fulfillment of the law. Jesus kept every single one of the commandments and became the curse. Make no mistake, the Law was a curse to us because we could never fulfill it. In Romans 8:2 it speaks about how through Christ, Christ was not Jesus last name Christ means anointed one in Greek meaning yoke obliterating power. Through the Messiah and his anointing, the law of Spirit who gives life has set you free from the law of sin and death". Galatians 3:13 Paul speaks about Jesus being made a curse, so we don't have to be. "Cursed is everyone who hung on a tree". Cross reference that with Deuteronomy 21:23. God never created us to live under the curse Romans 5:12 speaks about what happened to Adam and the earth when he fell. Genesis 3:19 says "by the sweat of your brow you will eat your food until you return to the ground".

God's intention for man and women was for them to have dominion, rulership, authority over the earth. God said in Genesis 1:26 "and let them have dominion". When Adam fell and disobeyed God, he gave the authority of the earth over to Satan. Proof of this is Matthew 4:9 Satan told Jesus to fall down and worship him and "All this power I give thee, and the glory of them: for that is delivered unto me; and to whomsoever I will I give it". Satan could not give something to Jesus he did not have legal authority over. This is the Gospel meaning good news in Greek that through Christ we have been redeemed from the curse empowered to fail and been put back into our rightful position to walk in The Blessing, meaning empowered to prosper Genesis 5:2; Genesis 1:28. To rule and dominate on this earth as Kings and Queens and all glory goes to Jesus Christ the anointed word of God GLORY GLORY GLORY.

Now religion has taught us the total opposite and that is our true enemy. Which is in operation of Satan and his demons all in the pursuit to lie to you and steal your birthright. This was the Jews viewpoint in John 8 the Jews refused the good news they could only see their religious viewpoints and the positions they held. The Jews argument was they were the only ones who could make the claim to be the children of God because of the Blood Covenant God and Abraham made in Genesis 15:9-21. The thing that the Jews were missing is this in Genesis 15:6 it says, "Abram believed the Lord, and he credited it to him as righteousness". So, Abraham received the promise because he held onto it and believed what he heard from God Genesis 12:2. In Galatians 3:29 it says "If you are born to Christ, then you are the true children of Abraham's seed, and heirs according to the promise. The promise was Jesus and he preached and taught about The Blessed life Matthew 5:1-10. If you are a born-again child of God, then that means Jesus came into your heart and you have been born again and The Blessing belongs to you through Jesus. The work he completed at the cross is available to you Now! According to John 10:10 . The problem is most of us have never been told who we are in Christ, so we suffer on this earth under the lies of the enemy who hides behind the doctrine of religion in plain sight.

Chapter 2

Rebellion

My sister Tierra Higgins was born January 28, 1989. She is one year older than me and, in every situation, she let me know. She was always into the extracurricular activities at school where she flourished. My sister had big dreams growing up. She would often say "I'm going to be a violinist, soccer star and if all else fails, an actress".

Growing up I could only see one purpose for my life and that was music. Music is so powerful because it can speak and reach people all over the world and ultimately connect them if only long enough for the song to be over. At the age of eight I began writing rock and roll lyrics filled with anger, regret, and hurt my way of expressing and releasing what was inside of me.

As a kid I had no idea what my mom was going through but as a mature Christian I now understand the devil and his attacks. My Mom was definitely dealing with possession and oppression especially since at that time in her life she had not accepted the new birth and been born again. I can remember weeks going by and my mom would just shut down and go into this catatonic state where she would not speak to me or my sister. This became the norm I would go downstairs, and all the lights would be off, and my mom would be sitting in utter darkness alone. The only resemblance of light would be from the cherry of her Marlboro cigarette reflecting off her face as she took a puff.

The one escape from the normal uncertainty I grew up with that I called a living hell was Fridays with my grandpa. His name was Jerry Eddy Higgins he stood six four with salt and pepper hair. He was a very monumental figure in my life, really the closest thing I had to a Father. He would pick my sister and I up after school and take us out to the movies and take us shopping and buy us whatever our little hearts desired. My Grandpa loved life and taught me one valuable lesson before he went home to be with the Lord. He told me "Kirk there is more to the world then the streets of Columbus Ohio never limit yourself".

I believe this is the mentality that has kept the poor under the curse over thousands of generations. Make no mistake poverty is certainly a curse just as well as cancer is a curse. Strokes, heart attacks and anything else that Jesus came to deliver us from when Adam fell. Jesus became the curse for us Galatians 3:13.

For a kid growing up in the streets the poverty mindset is something you accept; it is what shapes your reality. Until we renew our mind to the word of God our vision will always be our reality. It was once said to me like this, how can a little boy dream about a world greater than the one he sees? When the one he sees only goes as far as the corner store and back. My encouragement to the reader at this moment is dream. God told Abraham in Genesis 15:5 "if he could count the stars, 'so shall your offspring be". To that person living in poverty beneath what God best is for you in your life, stop looking at your situation, look towards heaven and start dreaming. The word of God is a promise to you if you are a born-again believer than your best life is right in front of you. Renew your mind to the word of God, believe it, start speaking it and you will see your reality change Romans 10:10.

I was the bad apple in the family always getting into trouble at school. It could have been because I was so restricted at home that when I got to school, I would just show off. I had absolutely no respect for authority. At home I felt like my mom was constantly trying to show me that she was the boss because I was the weaker one and that I had no choice but to obey. There was a lot of correction, but not a lot of love in our relationship. So, I began building walls up in my mind vowing that when I got older, I would not let anyone to control me.

This rebellious attitude started in kindergarten. I bit my teacher so bad she had to get a tetanus shot. I was always going along with the crowd, easily influenced by trying to impress people. One time in class me and another student were spitting spit balls. My Mom came into my kindergarten classroom and made me clean the entire school with a bucket of hot soapy water. My elementary years only fueled my rebellion. What I could not get away with at home I would get away with at school. I was constantly getting suspended for cursing out my teacher, being disrespectful, and fighting. One of the incidents included wrapping string around a bunch of chairs in pure boredom and almost tripping the teacher.

Now this was not an intentional act. All the hell we put this lady through, I do not blame her for taking it that way.

Halfway through my fifth-grade year. One of my partners put a razor blade in that same teacher's orange. From my understanding she quit and retired that day and never taught again. We were the worst class in that school, other teachers did not even like coming into our classroom. Makes me wonder if any of the teachers went home and prayed for us. Lord knows we needed it.

There was one teacher I did respect; his name was Mr. Mason. He took a strong liking to me and my artistic ability. He told me that if I stayed with it, I could get a scholarship for my drawing when I got older. It felt good having someone believe in me. My elementary school made the news at least 3 times that year. Teachers putting their hands on kids, kids putting their hands on teachers and Mr. Mason. He got accused of being inappropriate toward a girl in our class. It all came out to be a lie the mother put her daughter up to it just to sue the school. After the incident I begged Mr. Mason to come back but he said he just could not, his reputation as a man was questioned and that really hurt, I understood. I finished out the rest of my fifth-grade year watching Fox 28. We had substitutes every other day just to finish the school year out. The principle told my mom that I was only passing so they did not have to see me in their school the following year

Chapter 3

First God

Home life never got easier. As I got older the relationship with my mother only became more distant. I truly felt as a kid that my mom did not like me that she liked my sister better. So, I spent a lot of time in my room. My only source of love came from my Nana. I truly could do no wrong in her eyes, even though I always did, to her I was her baby.

I remember my first run in with the law. Me and a friend I hung out with in the neighborhood decided to put dog feces on my neighbor's porch. Of course, I got caught and the lady called the cops on me. My Nana wanted to believe the good in me so much that even when the cops showed up and she told them "I know he wouldn't do that". When I finally confessed, she was so hurt. Which was truly the only thing I felt bad about because I did not care about that lady's porch. Those oriental people treated me so badly and accused me of stealing their grandson's toys when I never did and even kicked me off their property. So, I felt justified in my actions, but seeing my Nana hurt like that hurt me. Not too long after that my Nana ended up moving to West Virginia to take care of her Mom Who had Parkinson's Disease. That is when I got more out of control.

I got introduced to drugs at the end of middle school. Weed was the answer to all my problems. This became the object of my obsession. My first God and if I can be completely transparent, I served my idol well. Some people would not consider weed that bad I did not at the time but make no mistake, weed is a mind-altering substance. Your mind is a makeup of what you put in it and what you put in it affects what you believe which is associated with the heart, better known as the spirit man. What you fill yourself up with is who you become. The bible teaches us to be sober minded: because our adversary the devil, as a roaring lion, seeking whom he may devour. He is not a roaring lion the scripture says, but I once asked myself after I became born again if I were in the jungle and there were lions seeking to devour me in what condition mentally would I want to be in?

Addiction is a terrible problem in our society, and it truly plagues us all Christians and non-Christians. The focus is mainly on the drug and a person's behavior being associated with the disease. I strongly disagree with that. The mind is where the disease takes hold and what you continue to put into the mind the heart will start believing, this is what shapes your belief system. To get true deliverance not that once an addict always an addict stuff they shove down your throat for you to regurgitate backup you must begin to download something different into the database. This is what the bible speaks about when the writers say to be renewed in the spirit of your mind Ephesians 4:23. This is what the original AA was founded on true deliverance. So, if you are reading this and are struggling with any addiction drugs, sex, porn, gambling whatever it is, you must begin to identify the lies that have been sown into you through information that you have downloaded. Then you must begin to change this information with new information. This new information will change your perspective which will change your truth which will produce a new reality. This does not mean that you will never have those thoughts or pictures pop up in your head again, but it does mean that when they come you do not have to come in agreement with them. How may you ask? By using words like a weapon. Words are the seeds that grow in us and produce whatever is behind those words. All information originates from a source and once you are able to identify the source than you can determine whether or not you want to draw from that source. To change what has been sown in we must begin to draw from a different source and dig up the information from the old. Words are the tools that dig up the lies in our minds.

I teach my clients that those thoughts are not theirs and they are only a byproduct of the information that has been downloaded through the five senses. The Bible speaks that we must hold every thought captive unto the obedience of Christ 1 Corinthians 10:5. This is the one scripture that freed me I realized that I could hold thoughts captive with words. Once I understood this I began to dominate over the lies of Satan and the pictures he tried to put in my head. This is my confession still today. Those are not my thoughts I do not listen to you or anything you have to say those pictures belong to you not me. I am a child a God and I do not think like that. Philippians 2:5 tells us that the mind that is in Christ Jesus we should let it be in us this is an act of our will we must let it be in us it will not automatically be there.

No this is not an overnight thing and dominating the thought life must become a part of a person's lifestyle to see real results. In Christ you will find that all the work has been done for you and all you have to do is receive your freedom. Without Christ a person must go at this on their own. If they remain free it will be done by trying hard and sheer willpower alone.

As long as you see yourself as an addict then that is what you will always be. In Christ we are not called to be addicts nor are you defined by past decisions. When we accept Jesus Christ as our personal savior, we believe by faith that we have been made the righteousness of God through Christ not addicts Mark 10:45.

Growing up my father was absent most of my life. Like I said previously, most of our relationship was based on empty promises over the phone. My Father would call and promise he was coming down to see me really soon. As a child I looked forward to these visits but as I got older, I realized there was no power behind those words. I do remember one time my mom took my sister and I down to Myrtle Beach to see my dad. I would say it was a joyous occasion. I could see that my mom and my dad did share a connection. My sister and I didn't share the same Dad, but my dad always treated her equally. I got to meet my younger brother when I went down there for the first time. His name is Mykiah Shenay and hear about another potential brother in Texas which ultimately turned out to be true, Jared. Unfortunately, Satan got a hold of him, and he is doing a life sentence behind bars.

I felt the need to paint this picture of my childhood to illustrate how the enemy begins to sow seeds into your garden. The garden I am speaking about is the mind. The bible says in 2 Corinthians 4:4 that Satan is the god of this world, and he has the minds of the unbelievers blinded so they cannot see the light of the gospel. Satan operates in the sense realm and begins to start shaping your belief system by your experiences and you gain experience through your five senses. The objects that Satan sows into your garden are not beautiful flowers or trees with ripe fruit on the branches. No, they are weeds designed to take over the garden and penetrate the heart till they get so rooted in you that they become who you are. The fruit is fear, hatred, anger, insecurities, doubt, unbelief, envy, strife, bitterness, hopelessness and many more and what your heart has an abundance of your mouth will eventually speak according to Luke 6:45. So from an early age Satan was programming my mind with his words and filling me up with his lies. The bible speaks about the importance of words. Our prayers are made of words and Jesus said in the sermon on the mount in Matthew 6:9-11 that we should pray like this. Religion has taught us to pray those exact words. That is not at all what Jesus was saying. He was saying when you pray pray in this fashion every time. Jesus called God Father being an example to us that as Jesus identified God as Father not ruler or judge, but Father so should we Galatians 4:6. Then He said hallowed by thy name, in the name of Jesus is the fullness of God. In the Greek hallowed means make holy, purity to venerate meaning only in the name of Jesus can you be made whole nothing missing nothing broken. Then Jesus said

Thy Kingdom come thy will be done on earth as it is in heaven. What Jesus is saying is when you pray, speak words that move heaven on earth. Your words are to bring God's will in heaven to the earth today. The same way you can come in agreement with God and speak His words the devil is trying to get you to speak the opposite. All through Proverbs the writer speaks all about words and the powers they contain for example proverbs 18:21.

Chapter 4

Body Bag

Your first example of a leader as a child is your parents. The Bible says in Proverbs 22:6 "train up a child in the way he should go; and when he is old, he will not depart from it". For the child to be trained this means that the ones doing the training must know the ways of God. The bible says that Jesus is the way and the light and that no one can come to the Father except through Him. Hebrews 11:6 says that without faith it is impossible to please God, because anyone who comes to Him must believe. I am convinced that most don't know the way even your average Christian is limited when it comes to revelation into God's word. They may be born again but they truly do not know their position in Christ and what is available to them. If they do not know then that means all they have is their own understanding which the bible urges us not to lean to. The way the bible is speaking about is through faith, and if we are not born again, we do not have this faith. If we are, we have been given the measure of faith but if it is never exercised it will not do us any good.

The Lord showed me something about the

children, they know how to believe. When we are kids, we believe the impossible. We have big dreams for our lives, and it takes someone to tell us that our dreams are not realistic for us to not believe them. So, we are taught how not to believe.

So, if the child is not trained according to God's word which is ultimately Gods will not unknown. Then his life will be one big example of leaning on his own understanding. This is unfortunately true for the saved Christian and the one who never accepts Jesus as their savior. Until we get revelation that God's word and God's will are one and the same, the bible will never come alive to us, and it truly has no power in our lives.

So, I can make the statement that I grew up under the roof of unbelief and people who raised me with their understanding. Which will always fail us and our children.

At the age of fourteen what was being downloaded, from an early age, into me turned into my reality. I left home believing that I was the best person to be in charge of my life. My mother always told my sister and I that when she was our age she was on her own and we could never do what she did. I was eager to prove my mom wrong that I could survive by any means necessary, and I didn't need anyone's help, especially not hers. It was later revealed to me that life is not about surviving it is about thriving.

Those of us who leave home early for a life of crime or grow up in the streets we are an example of that prodigal son the bible speaks about in Luke 15:11-32. We leave home because we do not believe that what is in the house (The Kingdom) is sufficient for our needs. The bible says in Colossians 1:13 that once we are born again, we are rescued from the dominion of darkness, and hath translated into the kingdom of his dear son. So, once we are born again, we are brought into the kingdom, but we leave home in search for a better way not knowing that everything we desire is in the house. Proof of this is in the parable Jesus said that the son went out and ended up a slave to a man who was a citizen to the country he was in. So, in the house he was an heir but leaving the house that same son becomes a slave. Religion has taught us that Christianity is about being a slave and that God is not concerned about your success but everywhere in the bible the Lord is making success stories out of all his prophets. Then the bible says he came to himself and repented the bible illustrates this not first in action but in thinking. "When he came to his senses, he said, " How many of my fathers hired servants have food to spare, and here I am starving to death! This is repentance, his mind begins to change about his situation. "I will set out and go back to my father and say to him: Father, I have sinned against heaven and against you". "I am no longer worthy to be called your son; make me like one of your hired servants". After all this changing of the mind (repentance) then the son got up and went to his father. The bible then says his father saw him and rejoiced and celebrated for his son was back and when he saw him, he didn't treat him like a slave he restored him to his rightful place he treated him like a son. The father opened the house and began to give him everything that was inside.

The bible speaks about the other son. He became jealous and even questioned his father saying all these years I served you and I never transgressed against you at any time, and you never gave me these things. The father's response was interesting. He said "Son, thou art ever with me, and all that I have is thine". This is religion you can be in the Kingdom and not be truly receiving the benefits as a son because you have been taught to see yourself and operate as a slave. Or you can be the son who leaves the house because religion has taught you to be a slave. You truly do not know that you are God's beloved son and everything that is in the kingdom is for you. I was the one escaping the slave lifestyle only to find out what true bondage was.

I spent all my time in this apartment complex called Carlin Manor, with a group of likeminded individuals mainly running the streets and getting into trouble. We would smoke weed all day and put our minds together on how we could get more weed and fulfill our desires. I remember dressing up in all black with two layers of clothes on feeling like I was invincible. These would be the nights that me and the group of guys that I ran the streets with, who I called my family, would go out and wreak havoc. Breaking into stores and vandalizing the community even tried to blow up a bus in a school parking lot. To be honest as much as we tried to pose a threat the biggest threat, we posed was to ourselves.

As a juvenile I spent a lot of time in and out of the court system in juvenile lock up on probation and in group homes. I truly had no vision for the future. My life was all about my loyalty and proving myself as a dependable soldier in the streets. Every time I would step in front of my juvenile judge, I would have a new case pending. My Mom did everything she could think of to correct my behavior, even trying to send me to West Virginia and enroll me in military school. Which was an utter failure seeing as how I could not even pass a drug test. Before we went, I told her I couldn't pass a drug test, so we went to the store that sold a drink to pass one. I ended up reading it wrong and instead of taking it eight hours before my test I thought that it had to be in my system for eight hours. So, what I was supposed to be peeing out to get clean became my sample. They had me pee in a cup and put my pee on the table next to all the other samples. The only difference is my pee happened to radiate the whole bathroom. It literally lit up the white walls of that bathroom. The guy came out and, in a country, voice said, "that boy just pissed neon". So, you can probably assume at this point military school was no longer an option for me.

When I came back, I was even more rebellious. I was a runaway living on the streets for months. The only time I would come back home is when the police brought me back. I got into a lot of crazy situations out there. One of the most dangerous situations consisted of getting beaten up by one of my running partners' whole family.

My friend's name was Mark, and we were both living on the streets at the time. We stayed at my friend Terence's house who went by T-Dogg. I was introduced to Mark's grandma prior to him running away but because I was on the run, I never gave anyone my real name. She knew me as Ryan. A week before Mark decided to go home and face the music, he went back to his house trying to snatch up his Xbox. While he was in the house his mom caught me in the backyard waiting on Mark and concluded that I was trying to rob the house.

The next week Mark turned himself in and went home. He snuck me in the house with him because for me there was no going back. After the cops showed up and cancelled the runaway report and asked a series of questions they left. Mark's grandma was off the chain to say the least she would ask Mark to do everything. The television remote would be right in front of her, but she would ask Mark to come all the way upstairs to get the remote that was literally inches away from her. So, within hours of being there he realized he made the wrong decision and with my help we were devising a plan to escape. He told his grandma that he was going upstairs to take a shower created a diversion while I snuck upstairs and the plan was for us to get on the roof, jump off and leave.

Everything worked to our advantage until we got on the roof. We were just about to jump off and we could hear his grandma screaming "Mark get back here". I truly thought we were in the clear. We jumped off the roof and opened the gate that went to the driveway, and I heard these words "Run Cuzz!" I did not know it, but Marks Grandma called his entire crazy family. His Uncle stepdad and Mother. I took off and jumped the fence going the opposite way and in midair felt a hand literally snatch me out of the air. My body came crashing to the ground and was met with a barrage of punches to the face. It was completely dark outside so every punch seems to come out of the darkness and just left me seeing stars. I was dragged in the house by my feet. I felt like I was in one of those scary movies where the killer is dragging his victim into a cellar or down into his lure to brutally murder him. I was grabbing onto whatever I could get my hands on to prevent my attacker from dragging me into that house. I knew if he got me in there it would be all bad for me. I truly did not know if I would be coming out the same way I came in BREATHING!

He did get me in there and immediately the same woman I saw a week ago asked me "why did you and my son try and rob my grandma's house"? Now it was all making sense they did not even know I was in the house the whole time. This was the same lady that saw me outside the house a week before and figured I had tried to come back to accomplish the job and her son Mark was in on it. The moment I spoke up and said "I wasn't "I was met with a stiletto heel rapidly moving toward my face. I moved out the way just in time and her heel went into the front of the kitchen cabinet I was thrown up against. She then told me "Do not lie to me again'. At this point I knew the only thing for me to do was to keep my mouth shut. A big black man proceeded to walk towards me as he knelt down. I could sense that this was the same man who dragged me in the house and snatched me over the fence. He grabbed me around my neck and proceeded to choke me, but the crazy thing is as he was choking me it was as if he was getting weaker. His grip was loosening as he was trying to apply force and he was falling backwards as he was trying to lean in. I knew at this time this was my opportunity to escape. I pushed him over, on his back, and tried to make a break for the door. I got up and proceeded to run toward the front door. I felt the knob of the front door. I was immediately met with a shoulder that slammed me into the wall and put me into a sitting position. Then a skinnier man grabbed me up, dragged me back into the kitchen where he pulled out the longest knife I had ever seen and ran it across his hand and said these words to me." You think you are crazy"; Up until this point I did believe that, but he was proven to fit the category more than me at the present time. "You think you are bad I cut your butt". This was interrupted by a knock on the door. It was the police. Man, I tell you what, I have never been so happy to see a police officer in all my life. He arrested me and I began to explain to him that I was in the house the whole time and my stuff was even downstairs in the basement. He could not deny what I was saying. I even told him I knew about them showing up and canceling the runaway report. Mark's mother and his other crazy family members did not buy it and were even more upset when the police officer said I would not be going to jail. The proof that I was allowed into their house and did not break in was downstairs on their basement floor.

As I look back on this situation, I do believe God was with me. There was nothing that was stopping that man from choking me out that night but with every bit of strength he used it seemed that he only got weaker and after that the attacks stopped. Not sure what really happened just know that something prevented him from hurting me any further. Then the words of the older man who pulled out the knife I could tell he was kind of perplexed as well. I did go
home that night and the police officer had a long conversation with my mother about my activity in the streets and how I was on the police officer's radar. His words" If your son doesn't slow down, you will be identifying him from a body bag".

This and other activities eventually led my judge to tell my mom to either find a place for me to go for the summer or she would. So, she called my dad and told him that if he did not come get me, I was going to be locked up in DYS. He came all the way down from Myrtle Beach South Carolina and drove me back with him. My Dad had no idea the kind of kid I was, but he would soon find out that I was more than he was ready to handle.

Chapter 5

At Peace

My Dad came down and picked me up in the most raggedy car I had ever seen. It was an old school Buick, and I was transporting an ounce of weed with me from Ohio to South Carolina. That was how our relationship really started off. When we got into South Carolina and to his apartment which he blamed me for losing he said bet you ain't never seen any weed like this before? I certainly had not and that led to me letting him know that I had something to smoke it out of which led to him asking me if I brought any weed down with me. I fessed up and showed him what I had. My Dad lost it. He started saying "we could have gone to jail; you could have got taken". I mean I thought you had like a joint or something know you bring enough dope to get me thrown in jail for ever". For me I truly could not have cared less, I was just ready to smoke.

Then there was the time I ventured out so far into the ocean past the buoys that I could not even be seen from dry land. My Dad was giving me the spiel about the ocean before I went in but for me all I could think about was escaping reality. As soon as he left and told me to have fun my mind was focused on one thing and that was swimming so far out into the ocean that nothing else was present. I accomplished this in a matter of minutes. I was so far out that the beach was close to not even visible. I could hear my dad screaming from the beach and as he screamed, I just went out further. I am not all the way sure where my head was at. I just felt the further I went the more distance I was putting between my problems. I began to drift on my back and stare up at the sky. Other than saying that prayer and accepting Jesus as my savior and welcoming Him into my heart at that bible study my sister and I went to when we were kids. This was one of the legit times I acknowledged that there was a God and He had to be real. Out there in the middle of the open sky surrounded by the vast open ocean I felt a connection to Him until a hand reached across my body and dragged me all the way back towards the beach. Needless to say, my dad was scared out of his mind he said, "are you crazy you could have died"? I was extremely mad because for once in my life I felt totally at peace and away from all my problems and my dad ruined it.

After about 6 months of us living together we began to grow distant from one another. My Dad stayed out drinking all night and I ran the streets getting into trouble, the same thing I did in Ohio. Eventually I began to build a reputation for myself, and it was imperative that I leave South Carolina. After less than a year of staying down there my dad put me on a Hooters airplane and flew me out of South Carolina back to Columbus Ohio to stay with my Mother.

Chapter 6

Church on the corner

This is the time in my life where the enemy truly had his claws in me. I was so lost, and I did not even know it. I was wrapped up in gangs, dropped out of High School and ran the streets smoking weed with my brother A.J.

Alexander Guzman better known as A.J He grew up with a similar story: the lack of love in the family led him to the streets.

The Lord has shown me without Christ it is truly impossible to love people. The best illustration that I can offer is 1 Corinthians 13. The bible says in 1 John 4:19 "we loved because He first loved us". Now I want to make this statement in clarity by no means am I speaking about the religious comments you hear on this subject. I am saying to have this love you have to have revelation (heaven revealed knowledge) that God is love and his desire is to love you. That is what John said in verse 16 "And we have known and believed the love that God hath to us". John was saying that this love was not a head knowing that this love was known and believed in the heart and to truly walk in that love you must have revelation of that love. We have desensitized love in this modern age down to a feeling. Love is not based on a feeling; love is truly a choice but because the English language is so condensed that we only have one word for love the moment we say it it loses its true value. In the Greek, the original text for the New Testament there are four words to express love: storge, philia, eros and agape. Agape is used to express the unconditional love of God for His children. Do you see that? Unconditional, a love that is not based on what you do but solely off of the person's choice to love you. This is the love that God not just possesses He is, the bible says He is love. This is the love that created you to walk in The Blessing and dominate on the earth. That same love is the love that went to the cross to redeem man from the curse. Sin, sickness, disease, and poverty that many Christians believe they have control over and continue to deal with on this earth. Religion has been preached to us over the pulpit by pastors who love God under the authority of Satan and his demons for so long that we have no idea the benefit of truly being a child of God and what Jesus really came to bring us or how much we are loved.

When you understand and believe the love that God has for you is real and that his sole purpose is to love you it is easy to give that love away because you walk around daily knowing in your heart that you are the object of his affection you truly are His beloved. According to Galatians 5:5 that love has been poured out into your hearts through the Holy Spirit, who has been given to us.

Then there's also the truth of love being a law in the kingdom and faith worketh by Love according to Galatians 5:6 and this is in correlation with 1 Corinthians

13. So, to give this love unconditional love not based on what someone can do for you or off of feelings you must be convinced of the love that God has for you. Then you choose this love by faith and operate in it because according to 1 Corinthians 13:13 the bible says "And now abideth faith, hope, charity, these three; but the greatest of these is charity meaning love and without love all the gifts of the Spirit will not work for us.

I am convinced this is the love that we are searching for. I call it a fulfillment of love, a love that takes nothing but gives everything. Most of us are broken and feel unfulfilled and run to the streets, relationships, people and even objects to fill that hole in us to try and complete the broken part of our hearts. In Christ you are fulfilled because once you become totally convinced about the love that God has for you you become whole, needing nothing else to complete you and whatever else you do find only compliments your completeness.

As two young men broken in a world controlled by fear A.J. and I did what we were taught to do, be criminals. We broke into everything that we could get into. If it was proven to be beneficial to our desire, we stole it. A.J. was a ladies' man all the women wanted him, and this always got him into trouble.

One situation I will never forget happened walking down 161 after just robbing someone's house. It was sunny outside, probably in the middle of June or July and A.J. and I were both on our way to one of our favorite hang outs Reflections on The Lake. This was one of the apartment complexes we would kick it at after we just robbed a house or if we needed a place to smoke weed and drink.

Now I must paint the picture because this time in my life I had no idea who I was or any knowledge of my true identity. Here we are two criminals walking down 161 I am sporting gang affiliated clothing with a blue bandana tucked into my left back pocket. A size 4XL blue T- shirt and a stolen .38 revolver on the side of my hip. A.J. was wearing an oversized blue T- shirt blue bandana carrying a .38 snub nose revolver and its broad daylight outside. When a black SUV pulls up beside us. The window rolls down and it is a middle-aged white lady behind the wheel. Immediately I feel as if this is a set up like she is trying to stall us here till the police surround us. So, the whole time I'm ready to leave but A.J. is standing over there falling for this stuff she is talking about. Saying she is opening up a new church on the corner of Karl and Cleveland Ave. and wants us to come. I am thinking like yea right lady I am not going to know church. While she continues to talk to A.J. about being saved and Jesus dying for him I am thinking this fool does not care nothing about knowing Jesus. Now I told yall I was not delivered yet. Eventually she gives my bro a pamphlet and rolls up the window and leaves and we continue back on the mission. I'm pondering this whole little altercation over in my head when A.J.'s voice interrupts my thinking. "Cuzz look at this" I look down and in the fold of the pamphlet she gave to him I see a folded up twenty-dollar bill. Now this truly left me perplexed. I could not understand why this Lady would stop two obvious thugs and give them money. We were definitely not hurting for it between us. We probably had at least two thousand dollars on us and that was just on our person. I began to try and rationalize it and there was no answer.

There were plenty of homeless people who could have used that money. We were thieves. Why give it to us? Then I heard a voice I never heard before say "I will Provide". I did not know this voice, but I knew it was not my own then I feeling I had not felt in a very very long time almost unrecognizable conviction. I looked over at A.J. and said "Cuzz we can't keep doing this".

I truly believe that lady was sent to us that day led by the spirit of God to sow that seed. As a man of God, I understand the law of sowing and reaping and that you sow where you want to go. So, for her to sow seed into my ground at that time I can only come to one of two conclusions: either she did not expect to receive back which is not operating in faith according to Luke 6:38 or the Lord led her to me to minister that message "I will provide." I am more inclined to believe the second scenario because the Holy Spirit continues to minster that message to me still to this day Amen. Thank God for the laborer's

The bible speaks about seedtime and harvest in Genesis 8:22. Some would compare it to your luck running out but seeing as how I am a faith man I do not believe in luck. Seedtime and harvest is based on a time period that the earth operates on as long as the earth endures and there is always a reciprocal for sin and not doing things God's right way. For the lifestyle A.J. and I lived there were only two options: jail or physical death and our time was running out.

Chapter 7

God's love

There we were sitting in the back of a police car after being pulled over while pulling into Allen's pawn shop in Westerville. I took the police on a foot chase that ultimately ended up with five cops running at me with nine millimeters being pointed in my direction. We were trying to pawn these coins off that we had stolen from somebody's house. Police pulled us over, found the guns and stolen property chased me down and took A.J. and I off to jail.

The girl who turned us onto the heist had her baby in the car which she ultimately lost custody of. I spent 10 days in the county to get out on a future indictment and was sentenced to 18 months of adult supervision. A.J. did six months in the county then six months CBCF which was a program to escape prison and seeing as how he had every felony count but F1 he definitely received God's mercy that day.

I want to make this point that God's mercy and God's blessings are two different things. I have heard people make the statement when God shows mercy on them that God blessed them or because they received a lenient sentence they got blessed. No, blessed means empowered to prosper God does not empower you to prosper when you are choosing death for your life. His mercy meaning goodness kindness is everlasting according to Psalm 136:24 "who remembers us in our low estate; for his mercy forever. In 2 peter 3:9 it speaks about God's attitude toward us and how he wishes for none to perish but for all to come to repentance.

Right after being released from jail for carrying a concealed weapon. I tried to break into a house and a lady was home with her kid. She chased me out of the house and three years later I was on the news with my face on the wheel of justice. Classified as Columbus most wanted.

So, I was on the run, my son's mother Brittany was pregnant with my soon to be first born son and within 4 months I was in jail. I ended up getting sentenced to 6 years in state prison a day after my son was born April 12th. I was sentenced to prison April 13th.

Pause, before you try and classify this book about a man who went to prison and later found out that prison was his biggest blessing let me stop the religious shenanigans. I used to believe that lie, even confess it out my mouth in ignorance. Then the eyes of my understanding were enlightened according to Ephesians 1:18. I began to understand that God is not the tempter for James 1:13 says "let know man say when he is tempted". That word tempted in the Greek means test a thing, make a trial, in a bad sense, enticed to sin. "I am tempted or tested of God; for God cannot be tempted with evil; meaning of a bad nature, neither tempteth he any man. God is not the tester, so he does not test or tempt. The enemy is classified as the tempter in Matthew 4:3 when he came to Jesus in the wilderness trying to test and tempt Him.

We must understand God's will for us is ultimately the best outcome. It is us that opens up the doors to allow Satan to wreak havoc in our lives. Or because of our lack of understanding we sit up under the waves of the storm instead of doing what Jesus taught in the Gospels Matthew 8:23-27; Mark 4:36-41; and Luke 8:22-25. First off Jesus was not concerned with the storm the scripture says He was sleeping resting not moved by what he saw in the natural. The bible talks about in various scriptures how we should operate today as believers that the just meaning righteous meaning God's right way of doing things shall live by faith Romans 1:17; Galatians 3:11; Hebrews 10:38; Habakkuk 2:4.

Jesus showed his authority by waking up and speaking directly to the storm in Mark 4:39 "He got up, rebuked the wind and said to the waves," Quiet! Be still!" Then the wind died down and it was completely calm". A lot of us are like the disciples sitting in the boat waiting the storm out or hoping someone else will help. Not knowing that you have all the authority in Jesus Christ and His anointing. You have been created to rule and reign, given authority to speak directly to those waves and say, "In the name of the Messiah and his anointing Peace be still!"

So, no prison was not an example of God's love or

God trying to sit me down. None of that hogwash religion teaches. I put myself there, the blessing is that God was with me. Prison is a terrible place and God does not desire for any of His children to go there but He will not force His will on us. People say there is nothing God cannot do that is a lie God cannot lie. The moment God lies he ceases to be God. The word says God is love that love is not forced because any love that is forced is not love. The bible says in Jeremiah 31:3 "I have loved you with an everlasting love; I have drawn you with unfailing kindness".

So, if you are one of those people believing that God will take you through the fire to get you to heaven ask yourself this? Is that really love, is that the unfailing kindness that is spoken in Jeremiah? No, it is not "It is the goodness of God that leadeth thee to repentance" Romans 2:4. Not the dope sick nights, or raids, or the cold concrete floors in the county jail or the homeless nights eating out of trash cans. I Don't know about you but none of those things sound like the goodness of God, at least not a God I want to follow.

Chapter 8

Sinner saved by Grace

I spent a couple months in CRC until I rode out to my parent institution Pickaway Correctional Institution. Whoever has done time behind bars you never forget your first day in prison. I Remember walking down the long dark hallways of D-Unit carrying a metal box with all my belongings in it. Walking by crash gate after crash gate with people passing by me in the hallway staring me up and down. Finally, I reached my destination. I walked into 7 bay prepared for whatever conflict awaited me. This was the nastiest place I had ever seen the paint was peeling from the black mold on the walls and the whole bay smelled like sweat from the two men doing pushups and pullups. Looking around I could tell that it was time to get

I stayed in D-Unit for about a month till I enrolled in a program called Oasis. Oasis was a Therapeutic drug program inside the prison in a completely different dorm. I enrolled in the program with the sole purpose to try and get out early. At this time, my son's mother and I were together and were betting on me not having to do all this time. I spent 6 months in the program the first time and left, came back the second time and spent almost a year there and eventually could not take any more. Oasis was the place where I began seeking God, but it was all in hopes to be a better person.

This is another one of those religious lies that we are just an old sinner saved by grace. If that be the case and we are just an old sinner then how can we be saved by grace? Grace is God's free gift unmerited favor in the area of loving kindness. In Ephesians 2:1-9 verse 8 says "for by grace are you saved through faith; and that not yourselves; the gift of God verse 9 says "Not of works, lest any man should boast". Romans 3:22 says "even the righteousness of God is through faith of Jesus Christ unto all and upon all them that believe for there is no difference." The difference Paul is talking about is between the Jew or Gentile. This righteousness means in the Greek God's right way of doing things remember it was counted toward Abraham for righteousness because he believed not because of his works. Your works will always be an example of your belief, but you must believe first. So, Jesus dying on the cross and becoming the curse for us paid the sin debt. He died for the sins of the entire human race 2 Corinthians 5:21 says "For He made Him," Who? God made Jesus sin who knew no sin to be sin for us, that we might become the righteousness of God in Him. Jesus laid down His life so we could in the eyes of God be seen as righteousness and God could treat us like we never sinned. In the words of my Brother Lank "Sin is what you do not who you are" the scriptures declare you are the righteousness of God by faith. The moment you get the revelation that Jesus delivered you from sin and make that your confession daily according to Romans 6:14 "sin shall not have dominion over you; for ye are not under the law, but under grace" sin will no longer be something you are dealing with sin will be dealing with you.

Once I left Oasis I went back to the basement. I did not end up in D-Unit this time I was moved to C-Unit which was downstairs from Oasis. This is not something I am proud of by any means, but prison life was easy for me. I was used to hustling and surviving so I picked up a hustle and started making hooch which is prison wine. My problem with authority always got me in trouble. I was never wise enough to keep my mouth shut. I had a chip on my shoulder and vowed I would not let anyone disrespect me. The bible speaks about this kind of person in Proverbs 12:15 "The way of a fool is right in his own eyes, but a wise man is he who listens to counsels. Proverbs 21:11" Simpletons only learn the hard way, but the wise learn by listening". Proverbs 19:29 "Judgements are prepared for scorners, and stripes for the backs of fools".

My lack of respect for authority eventually got me thrown in the hole. I cussed a correctional officer out and even threatened to beat him up. I served 14 days in the hole for this incident. I built a reputation on the compound for myself for being insubordinate and not knowing when to keep my mouth shut.

While being incarcerated I did accomplish more than just learning how to make wine and taking trips to the hole. I obtained my GED within three years of my incarceration as well enrolling in college. I completed the hours it took to get certified as a Chemical Dependency Counselor Assistant upon leaving prison.

My Son's Mother and I became distant after 2 years of me being locked up. I never blamed her. I understood she had to do what was best for my son Mason. I did have a faithful laborer in the Lord who continued to visit and speak life into me faithfully.

Lisi Cuckler is one of my mom's childhood friends who adopted my baby sister, Lexi. She would come and visit me and bring my son and my son's mother Brittany to see me. I could never understand why she would continue to fool with me. I mean I was a mess every time she would come see me, I would be cursing up a storm and talking all about prison life. She would ask me "Kirk what is your vision; your plan?" my response would be "I can't wait to put my feet on a real carpet, take a real shower". She would look at me and say, "what is that that's your plan?" It is amazing how we can have all this untapped potential and never see past our circumstances.

God created every man with a purpose, a gift to give to the world and unfortunately most of us die without ever fulfilling our purpose. I once heard Myles Munroe say it like this "the richest place in the earth is in the graveyards that is where the most untapped potential is some of the greatest symphonies never got sung some of the greatest books never got wrote and these people died never contributed to the world what God put inside them". Listening to this message and many other anointed Men of God was one of the things that encouraged me to write this book. In Genesis 1:11 God spoke about the earth bringing forth seed after its own kind, and the tree yielding fruit after its kind and God saw it good. The thing that speaks to me is when God recreated creation He never had to go back to the soil because the creative ability was inside everything He created. We are just like the land; everything we need, every creative ability is inside of us because God put it there. The vision you have comes from God but if you do not believe in the vision, you will never see what God saw when he put it there, Good. The bible says in Proverbs 18:16 "A man's gift maketh room for him, and bringeth him before great men".

I truly want to encourage my reader right now. If you are a born-again tongue speaking child of God, you were created to dominate. Not work at know dead end job making pennies for the rest of your life. You have something to offer this world and your purpose is hidden in Christ the more you seek Him and His anointing all things become possible Matthew 19:26. Find A promise in the Bible begin to declare it over your life every day, stand on it in faith with revelation and see if God does take you to places you could only dream of 2 Corinthians 1:20 "For all the promises of God in Him are yes, and in him Amen, to the glory of God by us."

Chapter 9

"Bump Joseph"

After six months of being out the hole from an incident that I technically could have got rode out to a higher-level security prison. I got accepted to work outside the fence. This is a privilege in prison. It allows you to work at a job, make better pay and stay in a cleaner dorm. I had my mind on something totally different. Tobacco is a big money maker in prison especially since they took smoking out the joints so the moment, I got accepted I had my mind on one thing, money.

In 1 Timothy 6:10 the bible speaks about the love of money being the root of all evil, but money is not, it is the love of money. God created you to be prosperous, that is The Blessing. Not just in money, in every area of living but glory be to God it's in money too. In Genesis 12:1-2 God promised Abraham if he would get away from his kindred and from his father's house to the land God showed him God would make him a great nation and bless him, make his name great; and thou shalt be a blessing. In Genesis 13:2 it says "And Abram very rich in cattle in silver, and in gold. Jesus Christ laid his life down the bible says in John 10:18 to deliver us from the curse. Galatians

3:18 "Cursed everyone that hangeth on a tree". Poverty is sure enough a curse and if you do not believe that you aint experienced it yet. No one that was in the bible, Old Testament prophet or new was broke not even Jesus. In 2 Corinthians 8:9 Paul says "For we know the grace of our Lord Jesus Christ, that, though He was rich, yet for your sakes He became poor, that ye through His poverty might be rich. People make the statement I do not need all that money. I am good as long as I have enough for me and my family this is a false sense of the word humility. My pastor makes this statement "If all you want is enough for you and yours that is not humility that is selfishness". That is not God's plan. He Blessed Abram to be a blessing and to take that blessing everywhere he went.

Now in my situation I was not seeking the Lord and it was all about personal gain. Money had become my God but make no mistake the God of the bible is a prosperity God. If you operate lawfully in the Kingdom, you can surely expect for the Blessing to overtake you Deuteronomy 28:2.

God has sent many prophets my way throughout my life. Earthly words cannot truly express what they mean to me and how thankful I am for the seeds they have planted in my heart. Lank is one of those prophets. I used to watch one of my brothers from Oasis named Mack walk the track on the compound with this brother Lank. I would pass them by walking the track by myself plotting on ways to get tobacco in the institution. It always confused me when I would overhear their conversations. They were always talking about God every reck period all day long. In my carnal mind all I could see was this older man who had been down for a while kicking it with my dude who was younger. Which in the joint really is not a good look. My conclusion was this old man is trying to drape my dude off with the word of God meaning some homosexual stuff was going on here. Paul speaks about in Romans 8:7 how the carnal mind enmity against God. Then Paul says in 1 Corinthians "But the natural man receiveth not the things of the Spirit of God: for they are foolishness unto him; neither can he know, because they are spiritually discerned. Little did I know I was bumping into the Kingdom of God.

There was one brother that was in prison with me. I went to school with on the outs (slang for free world) that I truly respected. My brother still to this day Garret Jones we call him G. The people in prison that followed God were corny to me. My dude Mack would always try and preach to me when he was not kicking it with Lank about Jesus. My response would be "When I see you on the streets and I pass you this nine pack (drugs) tell me about Jesus, when I see you on the streets and I tell you about this 50,000-dollar lick (robbery) tell me bout Jesus I aint trying to hear bout know Jesus now". I respected G though. His walk with God was different. I could tell it was genuine and his mindset and sense of security intrigued me.

Lisi would never tell me when she was going to visit me, she would always surprise me. She later told me that she never wanted to tell me she was coming because if something happened and she could not make it she would be letting me down. She would rather it be a surprise. So, when she brought my older sister Tierra with her to come see me that was even more of a surprise. The visit was the same as usual. Lisi preached to me how she wanted me to be like Joseph in the bible and rise to the top. My response would be: "You don't know what I go through in here, the CO's talk crazy to you, bump Joseph I'm ready to crash out!". My sister was trying to talk to me too but when I say I was a fool I was the smartest fool ever.

At this time in my incarceration, I was heavily involved with the tobacco trade. I was sending home at least three hundred dollars a day. I lied to Lisi about what I was doing and had her doing a lot of stuff that if she knew the truth, she never would have agreed to it. I later came clean about all of it and apologized for deceiving her.

My brother G kept hounding me about letting him talk to my sister over the phone. Now anyone else I wouldn't even consider it but he kept on about it and would say "I just want to talk to her about God".

My sister had always been into God ever since we got saved at this bible study thing we would go to during the summer as little kids. I was actually in her car a week before I got caught for the charge that initially put me in prison. Right before I got out of the car, she looked over at me and said, "Kirk I know why your life is the way it is" I said, "Oh you do enlighten me" and she said, "it's because you don't know God." I looked her straight in her eyes and said, "F God I'm out here and I don't see God". It was not that I didn't believe God was real, it was just that I didn't think He cared about me. My mentality was this: if He was not concerned about me then I was not concerned about him. Man, how we can be so wrong.

I eventually gave G the number to get him off my back. I really believed he was genuine about just wanting to talk to her about God. They did start talking. My sister was trying to get G to get me to go to a bible study, I later found out. G approached me that same week I gave him the number, after breakfast in the gym about coming to a bible study with him. If it was anyone else, I would have told them to kick rocks, but I respected G, so I went. A white guy named Shawn Nightingale was running the bible study. My first experience, it was cool. I kind of liked it besides all the hugging and everyone calling me brother. I started going every day after breakfast. Little did I know that this would be the series of events that would change my life forever

Chapter 10

Embryo Stage

"Does anyone know anything about speaking in tongues?". This was the discussion for today in bible study. Individuals in the group started raising their hands speaking what they thought and their own personal opinion on this subject. "A Puerto Rican brother raised his hand and started talking about his baby brother receiving this gift on the outs having only stepped into a church one time. He said, "My pastor started praying for him and 'BOOM' next thing you know he just started speaking in another language uncontrollably". Then he said "this really made me question God. "Why did he receive, knowing nothing about God but I go to church every Sunday and I have never done this"?

I was just about to raise my hand and give my opinion on this subject which for the record does not mean squat and has no power when it comes to God's word. The quickest way to show you are unskilled in the word of God is by this statement "This is what I think it means". Sorry to burst the religious bubble but the word of God is not meant for your interpretation. It does not mean what you think it means it means what the writers intended it to mean. Paul wrote in 2 timothy 3:16-17 "All scripture is God-breathed and is useful for teaching, rebuking, correcting, and training in righteousness,17 so that the servant of God may be thoroughly equipped for every good work. Paul also wrote in 2 Timothy in 2:15 "Study to shew thyself approved unto God, a workman that needeth not to be ashamed, rightly dividing the word of truth". If Paul wrote to Timothy urging him to rightly divide the word of God well then this would mean that you can divide the word wrongly as well. Paul says needeth not to be ashamed, that is what happens when we try to interpret the scriptures according to what we think. The word of God is powerful according to Hebrews 4:12 means it is active, it is not just a feel-good message or a fairy tale its real and in operation today. When we do not use it skillfully, rightly dividing the word of truth then it won't work for us. It may sound good, that is what religion does, it sounds good, but there is no power, no anointing present. Religion will lead you into bondage, toiling for your salvation opposed to receiving the blessed gift by faith Ephesians 2:8.

At this time, I was in the embryo stage of my Christian walk, so I had no understanding or revelation regarding the truth. My next comment was going to be "I think this is a gift that God chooses those he wants to receive". Which is a lie from Satan himself and I truly intend on proving this later in the book. Allowing the word to be confirmed out of the mouth of two or three witnesses 2 Corinthians 13:1. Scripture on top of scripture rightly dividing the word of truth.

The moment I began to open my mouth. I was immediately stopped by a calming yet more powerful voice than I have ever heard. That almost sounded audible to me. I heard it plain as day "NO WORD ESCAPES MY LIPS"! I had no idea what this meant but I felt this overwhelming sense of comfort and love. It was like someone opened up the sun inside of me and all the light came in. It truly was amazing, a feeling I had never felt in all my life. I raised my hand and stammered out "I think, I mean, I think God just spoke to me". It was as if everyone else knew it too. I could not fight the smile on my face from spreading from ear to ear. Shawn the guy who ran the bible study class looked at me and said, "What did he say"? I repeated the words I heard so plainly "NO WORD ESCAPES MY LIPS". He looked at me and said "What does that mean "? I said, "I don't know" Everyone went back to the discussion but from that moment I was forever changed. My seeking would begin, and I needed answers.

Chapter 11

Why would God choose me?

I left out of that study with more questions than answers. "Was that really God and if so, why would He speak to me?" There are plenty of people who spend their entire life seeking God and never have that kind of experience. I wondered if God needed me for something. I could not wrap my little peanut brain around this. Of course, doubt started sneaking its way in "you tripping God ain't speak to you". No matter how many voices came into my head I knew what I knew God spoke to me period. The next day I went to bible study. Shawn was having it in a different room. As soon as I walked in there, who did I see? It was the old dude Mack would always talk day in and day out about God. Something in me told me he would have the answers that my spirit longed for.

Lank is a brown skin brother that stands about '5 '5 pretty well built from many years of incarceration. He keeps a smooth bald head with a long Moses like beard.

I walked up to him and said, "What up Lank"? He said, "What up lil bro"? He was leaning against a stack of chairs apparently waiting for the session to start. I looked at him and said, "I got to holla at you big bro". He said, "okay let's roll". As soon as we stepped out of the building, I started in. I began to tell him everything that had my mind so perplexed. The main question that truly was bothering me the most was "Why"? Why would God choose me to talk to? I had gone over this and over this in my head and the only conclusion I could come to was that God needed me. When I would talk to anyone else about this conclusion, they would tell me "God don't need no one He is God" Not Lank though He looked at me and said, "I agree lil bro".

For years religion tried to talk me out of the conclusion I came to when I heard God's voice. Many people would tell me God does not need nobody, it's us that needs Him. Now I am not in disagreement with that in any way. I wake up every morning and declare the word of God over my life. He ultimately is my source. When I say that I do not mean those old religious prayers either. "OLE GOD thank you for this air and the fact that I'm here and you rescued an old sinner like me" No, what I mean when I pray the word of God, I mean just that I pray His word back to him. I pray His perfect will over my life. Now you may ask how can I know His will for my life when His will is unknown? Simple because his will is not unknown. 1 John says in 5:14-15 "And this is the confidence that we have in Him, that, if we ask anything according to his will, he heareth us." So, if God's will is unknown to man then we should have no confidence in God hearing us. Praise God His will is not unknown because His will and His word are one and the same. 1 John 5:15 says "If we know that he hears us, whatsoever we ask, we know that we have the petitions that we desired of him". So, to have confidence that God hears us we must ask according to his will and to ask according to his will we must know His will. Then with this confidence we know that we have whatever we asked for. Not convinced? We'll let the word be established then, in God's will it says "Therefore I say unto you, What things soever ye desire, when you pray, believe that ye receive, and ye shall have them Mark 11:24. Are y'all getting anything out of this? If it's in His word in the form of a promise, it's His will for you to have it. All you have to do is what the word says do and believe God for it Amen.

I know I have been feeding you guys a lot of meat throughout the pages of this book, and it may be hard to swallow it all. I have said some things that may have you questioning everything you have ever been told about Christianity, Good. I do believe that is the Holy Spirit's intended purpose and with his leading I do not intend on stopping now.

Back to my conclusion, God needed me. Before you get to shouting me down cause I'm talking real good let me make my case.

That is a comment my pastor makes and one I have heard a Great Man of Faith Kenneth E. Hagin make many times. If you don't know about Kenneth Hagin I encourage you to check him out, sure enough the truth.

So, let us go back to God's intended plan for man. To do that we must talk about a topic you will only hear in a faith church or around the anointing THE BLESSING. Now I know I have spoken about The Blessing in chapters past and guess what I am going to keep talking about it. For two reasons religion has kept it from us for so long and it is just so good Hallelujah. In the first book of the bible Genesis, it explains how God recreated the earth by faith. Genesis 1:2 says "The earth was without form, and void; and darkness upon the face of the deep. And the Spirit of God moved upon the face of the waters. That without form and void in the Hebrew means "tohu va bohu" means waste and empty total waste land a place of chaos. God never created the earth in this fashion. Ask yourself why would a God that characterizes himself as light create something that is his polar opposite darkness? The answer is because he did not. The prophet Isaiah spoke about God's intention for creating the earth. Isaiah 45 says in the NLT version "For the Lord is God, and he created the heavens and earth and put everything in place. He made the world to be lived in, not to be a place of empty chaos. "I am the Lord, "he says, and there is no other. Now why was the earth in this fashion? Lucifer was on the earth before man was created. He had a throne in the earth and the earth was inhabited. There were birds and animals, dinosaurs to be exact and other beings on the earth before man was ever created. Lucifer was in control of it all. Ezekiel 28:15 explains what happened to Lucifer "You were blameless in your ways from the day you were created till iniquity was found in thee." In the Hebrew that word iniquity means unrighteousness, wrong, deviate from, in act and speech. In Isaiah 14:13 the prophet Isaiah said, "For thou hast said in thine heart, I will ascend into heaven, I will exalt my throne above the stars of God." For Lucifer to ascend into heaven means he had to be on the earth. The prophet Isaiah said Lucifer said in his heart he would take his throne and exalt lift it up above the stars of God. Lucifer's plan was to take his throne on the earth and overthrow God. Jeremiah explains in chapter 4 what he saw in the spiritual realm after Satan went against God. The mountains trembled, there was no light and all the birds of the heavens fled. Jeremiah said in verse 25 "I beheld, and lo, there was no man, reading on down to verse 26 it says, "and all the cities thereof were broken down". Lucifer was in the earth and had ownership over all the creatures inhabiting it until he went against God. God then removed His life-giving spirit from the earth. This is what made the earth "tohu va bohu" an utter waste land, complete darkness.

God's Spirit moved Hebrew word for hovered upon the face of the waters. God did not speak what he saw, this is the God like faith Romans 4:17. He spoke light into the darkness. "God said, let there be light: and there was light. I heard it like this: LIGHT BE and LIGHT WAS. Hebrews 11:3 says "By Faith we understand that the universe was created by the word of God, so that what is seen was made from the things that are not visible. The Bible does not say that the earth was created out of nothing, it says it was created out of what could not be seen, what could not be seen was substance, that substance is faith according to Hebrews 11:1 "Faith is the substance of things hoped for, the evidence of things not seen". So, faith is not your belief in God and believing in his existence. God revealed it to me like this faith is assurance based on what God has spoken and hope or expecting to see those things even though they contradict what can be seen or experienced with the five senses. Abraham exercised and used this faith to access the promises that God made to him in Genesis 17:4. Romans talks about how Abraham considered not his own body but was assured of what God spoke to him even though it contradicted what his natural situation and circumstances said was possible " And being not weak in faith, he considered not his own body now dead, when he was about an hundred years old, neither yet the deadness of Sara's womb"

God created the earth and with the word of God mixed with faith everything was created. St. John 1:1-4 "In the beginning was the Word, and the Word was with God, and the Word was God. 1:2 "the same was in the beginning with God".1:3 All things were made by him: and without him was not anything made that was made".

God created man in His likeness and formed his body from the dust of the earth. Then breathed the breath of life into that dirt body and he became a living soul. In the Hebrew breath of life means divine inspiration the life-giving ability to create by what he breathed out. Adams' job was to recreate the earth by the creative force in his mouth. Do not believe it? Man was created in resemblance of God. God is a spirit we are a spirit every spirit has a soul mind will and emotions and God put all of that in a physical body to operate in the earth. Then gave man every ability to rule and reign on the earth by modeling after his creator. God is a speaking God and He created everything with divine inspired life creating words. Proverbs 18:21 says "Life and death are in the power of the tongue, and those who love it will eat its fruit". That word tongue is translated in the Hebrew organ of speech or spoken words. Adam was to act as God on the earth and use the divine inspired life creating ability that was given to him to create life. In Romans 4:17 Paul wrote "even God, who quickeneth the dead, and calleth those things which be not as though they were". Adam was to model after his father and speak life to dead things call those things that be not as though they were by faith. Jesus was the greatest example of this. Jesus only spoke what the Father told Him to say he never agreed with the circumstances know matter what the facts said. He spoke those things that be not as though they were. That was the mandate given to Adam and through Jesus that is our orders today. Your biggest weapon is in your mouth and what you say you will have according to Mark 11:23 "he shall have whatsoever he saith".

In Genesis 1:26-28 God said, "let us make man in our image, after our likeness: and let them have dominion". He gave man the authority over the earth. In verse 28 it reads "AND GOD BLESSED THEM." Deuteronomy 28 speaks about these blessings. Adam's job was to make the rest of the world look like the garden of Eden with the power of The Blessing.

God empowered man to prosper in every area of living that is The Blessing. Deuteronomy 28 speaks about these blessings which are a byproduct of The Blessing. God created the Garden and everything in it in six days on the seventh He finished His work and rested. The first thing God gave man was purpose. In Genesis 2:15 "The Lord God took the man and put him into the garden of Eden to dress it and to keep it". Adam's purpose or assignment was to make the rest of the world look like the Garden of Eden which operated under the kingdom of heaven. The moment Adam fell and turned the authority of the earth back over to Satan. The Blessing turned into the curse Deuteronomy 28:15. The complete opposite man was empowered to fail in every area of living Romans

5:12. This kicked God out of the affairs of the earth because He gave man authority over the earth and man gave it legally over to Satan. Proof of this shows up in the wilderness when Satan tries to tempt Jesus. Satan told Jesus in the Gospel Luke 4:6 "All this power will I give thee, and the glory of them: for that is delivered unto me; and to whomsoever I will give it". The moment man fell God had a plan to get The Blessing back into the earth and redeem man to his rightful position. God is a Spirit according to John 4:24 and a spirit does not have legal authority in the earth. Same way Satan needs a body to fully operate in the earth, so does God. That is why God made a covenant with Abraham. Genesis 12:1-2 says, "Now the Lord had said unto Abram Get thee out of thy country, and from thy kindred, and from thy father's house, unto a land that I will shew thee." Verse 2 speaks of the promise God made to Abram "And I will make of thee a great nation and I will bless thee and make thy name great; and thou shalt be a blessing". God's intention was to bless Abram so he could be a blessing and take that blessing wherever He was called to go.

God made a covenant with Abraham so He could get back into the earth. This covenant gave God legal authority back into the affairs of man and allowed God to operate in the earth lawfully. In verse Genesis 17:1-27 speaks about the promises God would fulfill in his covenant with Abraham and his descendants. Galatians 3:29 says "and, if ye be Christs then are ye Abraham's seed, and heirs according to the promise. If you are in Christ, then you are justified by faith and that makes you the seed of Abraham meaning all those promises in that Covenant belong to you through Jesus. Galatians 3:7

"Know ye therefore that they which are of faith, the same are the children of Abraham."

So, does God need you? Yes, he does. Since the moment God reached into the earth and formed man and breathed Spirit filled words into him, He has had purpose for man. To love him and use him to rule and dominate the earth. Adam dropped the ball according to Romans 5:12 "Wherefore, as by one man sin entered into the world, and death by sin; and so death passed upon all men; for that all have sinned:" Christ redeemed us Romans 5:17 "For if, by the trespass of the one man, death reigned through that one man, how much more will those who receive God's abundant provision of grace and of the gift of righteousness reign in life through the one man, Jesus Christ!" Romans 5:19 "For just as through the disobedience of the one man the many were made sinners, so also through the obedience of the one man the many will be made righteous". Paul wrote in 1 Corinthians 15:45 "And so it is written, the first man Adam was made a living soul: the last Adam was made a quickening spirit". It is because of the second Adam we can receive the new birth. Jesus spoke about this new birth in John 3:3 "Jesus answered and said unto him, Verily, verily, I say unto thee, except a man be born again, he cannot see the kingdom of God". When we accept Jesus as our savior and make Him Lord over our life our dead spirit gets reborn again and we become a new creation. We are delivered from the power of darkness Satan and the curse, and hath been translated into the kingdom of his dear Son According to Colossians 1:13.

Jesus delivered us from the curse of the law of sin and death. Jesus endured the punishment for the entire human race to put man back in right standing with God so God could treat man as if he never sinned. 2 Corinthians says, "God made him who had no sin to be sin for us, so that in him we might become the righteousness of God". This is God's intended purpose for man to love him like a son or daughter and bless him or her to be blessing. It was the promise God told Abraham. The same promise God gave to the children of Israel. It is the reason Jesus Christ came into the earth; it is the Gospel.

Every parable Jesus ever taught in the gospels was about the kingdom. The abundant overflowing life is in the kingdom and the Kingdom is now! In Luke 17:21 it says "Neither shall they say, Lo here! or, lo there! For behold, the kingdom of God is within you". Translated in the Greek means in the midst of you. In Matthew 3:2 John the Baptist preached "Repent, for the kingdom of heaven is at hand. John the Baptist's whole message was about repentance to prepare the people's hearts for the Messiah and His anointing. What did Jesus preach and teach about? God's jurisdictional authority of heaven on the earth THE KINGDOM. In Matthew 11:12 Jesus said, "And from the days of John the Baptist until now the kingdom of heaven suffers violence, and the violent take it by force". God has a specific assignment in the earth for every believer and you are to operate under heavens authority to fulfill it. Whatever it is God has called you to do the moment you got born again and baptized in the Holy Ghost you have been given power to complete this assignment through the anointing. That assignment is to take the blessing and create the garden of Eden wherever you go using God's authority on earth (The Kingdom). To operate in this authority, you must have revelation on how the kingdom works which will only come by hearing the accurate word of God. You must get disconnected from the spirit of religion and this Babylonian system and get connected to the anointing. Men and women of God who are preaching and teaching on prosperity. Yes, I said it prosperity, you were created to prosper in every single area of living spirit soul and body. This is our birthright, this is the good news, this is the Gospel, this is God's plan for the sons and daughters of God, and he needs you to fulfil it. Romans 8:22 "For we know that the whole creation groaneth and travaileth in pain together until now." Creation is literally groaning in pain waiting on the manifestation of the Son of God. For us to rise up and take back what belongs to us. We are to rule and reign on this earth over Satan and his demons and God needs you to do it.

Chapter 12

God Speaks

If you ever would have told me I would give up everything in pursuit of Christ I would have told you, you got the wrong guy. I cannot speak for anyone else but from the moment He revealed Himself to me I fell in love. His words intrigued me so much it became my answer, my source, my everything. It took some years for the revelation to come regarding those words I heard that day in bible study "NO WORD ESCAPES MY LIPS". The word God was speaking about was His word. In Matthew 16:13 Jesus asked His disciples, "whom do men say I am"? In verse 14 the disciples respond, "Some say thou art John the Baptist: some Elias; and others Jeremias, or one of the prophets". In verse 15 Jesus said "But whom say ye that I am? In verse 16 Peter said, "Thou art the Christ, the Son of God". In verses 17-18 Jesus said, "Blessed art thou Simon Barjona for flesh and blood hath not revealed unto thee: but my Father in heaven". What was revealed? Peter got revelation that Jesus was the Messiah that the prophets had spoken about Isaiah 61:1 "The spirit of the Lord God is upon me; because the Lord hath anointed me to preach good tidings unto the meek; he hath sent me to bind up the broken hearted, to proclaim liberty to the captives, and the opening of the prison to them that are bound". Then Jesus confirmed it in Luke 4:17-19. Christ was not Jesus last name Christ means anointed in the Greek. Jesus Christ was the promised messiah the anointed one to preach the gospel to the meek, the poor, the wealthy, and the afflicted. Jesus was sent to bind up the brokenhearted, proclaim liberty to the physical and spiritual captives, and to open the eyes of those who are bound. What does the anointing do? It breaks the yoke, it breaks the chains of bondage, it sets you free and He who the Son sets free is free indeed John 8:36. It is the yoke destroying yoke obliterating power of God. This is the rock Jesus told Peter He would build his church on, and the gates of hell would not prevail verse 18. That rock was not Peter, it was revelation knowledge from Heaven of who Jesus is. I believe with everything in me God spoke audibly to me that day. After years of studying on this and meditating on these words. The one thing I am sure of is that these are the exact words that led me to Christ and broke the chains.

I remember sitting on my bed praying telling God I loved Him, and I trusted Him. At this time, I was still hustling. The people I had helping me on the street, bringing me the tobacco went AWOL, and I was plotting on my next move. My son's mother was not doing good out there and all I could think of is I got to make something shake for her and my son. In the middle of my prayer the Lord stopped me and said, "you don't love me, and you don't trust me". Plain as day just like that. He showed me this picture of two giant hands and a person falling into those hands. Then He said, "When you fall back you don't look back at the hands that's behind you;

you just fall back and trust in the hands that's holding you up". When I heard that I was stuck then he said, "you don't love me and you don't trust me".

That was the day I said to myself "I am standing in the way of something greater than myself" and I gave up hustling for good. It is funny how God works the first time I talked to Lank I told him "I need answers'" He said if you sacrifice the time, I will sacrifice the time". As soon as he said that the first thing that popped in my head was "this aint that". I ain't bout to be walking the track with you like Mack did every day. Did I mention God is funny, that is exactly what I did day in and day out I gave up everything voluntarily for that word.

Since then, God has revealed to me what He was really saying to me that day on my rack. In 1 John 4:19 John says, "We love him, because He first loved us". In verse 16 John talks about knowing and believing this love. This is not just the religious knowing and believing this is a revelation of God's love. This is the knowing and believing that in every situation God is for you and desires the very best for you. In Isaiah 54:9 Isaiah is recorded here saying that God has sworn to never be wroth or angry with thee, nor rebuke or express sharp disapproval or criticism of or because of your actions.

What God was really saying to me that day was Kirk you do not know how much I love you and because you do not know how much I love you it is impossible for you to trust me.

God revealed many truths to me about the kingdom through my brother Lank on that track. He would teach me about the character of the man of God. He once asked me "Lil bra do you really believe you are a new creation in Christ?" I did not have an answer for him in those days but his reason for asking resonated so much to me. He would say "When I found out that I am a new creation in Christ I believed I had a whole new life. Meaning the old Lank is dead and I am a completely different person. Where I once would be lazy, I would be diligent. Where I once would be disrespectful and prideful, I would be humble and genuine." Conversation's day in and day out like these were the very building blocks that God used to reshape my thinking. I ain't going to lie to you I was a hot mess in those days, from losing jobs to cursing inmates and CO's out you name it. Those walks around that track always brought me to the light and afterwards I would go back to my rack and get in the scriptures. I remember one time I told Lank "sometimes it's hard to get in the word or I forget" His response was so heavy that most Christians today would not be able to handle it. He said, "That's because it isn't real to you yet, lil bra you don't forget to breathe, until the word becomes like breathing for you it will never be real to you." Today I can say I honestly understand exactly what he was talking about. Until you see the word as life it will never work for you and never hold the value it is intended to have in your life as a believer. Near the end of our sessions walking the track right before the CO's would shut the yard down for the night. I would always look at him and say, "We are on the road again, Lank." He would look at me and say, "What Road?" I would say "The Road to Damascus." He would laugh and say, "Yeah Lil bra The Road to Damascus."

Chapter 13

"Speak Lil Bra"

I will never forget the day I was baptized in the Holy Ghost. Oh, I know there are some of you that believe this is a gift that some receive, and some do not it is all in the mysterious will of God. I have covered in previous chapters how God's will is not mysterious to us. His will and His word are one and the same. I pray you get that revelation. When I truly understood that it changed the way I viewed the Bible forever.

I could not wait to get to this part of the book. This is an area a lot of Christians are lacking in and it is because religion has once again lied to us. First, I will tell you my experience then I will tell you the truth regarding this wonderful prayer language to God.

At this point I would meet with Lanky Lank (that is what we called him) every day after breakfast in the gym. This day I really had something to discuss with him. The day before I experienced a supernatural feeling while praying for a brother in the bible study group I now attend regularly. I put hands on him and started praying and I felt a feeling come over my body. I started shaking and my eyes started fluttering till the point I had real tears coming down my cheeks. Now I was not mature enough in the Word to go and find the answers to the questions I had, nor did I really believe that they were in there. In the beginning Lank was my source. He was a good teacher because he always pointed me back to the word

I want to say this to my reader: if you are being discipled by a Man of God never let him become your source. If he or she is truly called by God to play that position in your life, they should always be encouraging you to get in the word and hear from God for yourself. Never replace God with man, you are His sheep, and He does speak to you John 10:27-30. Teachers are there to teach and show you how to accurately divide the word of God but not replace God in your life.

As soon as I saw Lank, I started in "big bro I think I felt the Holy Spirit". He said, "Ok what happened"? I began to tell him about my experience from the previous day. After I finished, he looked at me and said, "What do I always tell you"? Now you got to understand something about Lank when he asked me a question, he never gave me the answer. This is one of the things I valued about our conversation the most. He would always tell me "My job is not to tell you what I know, my job is to make you think and study so you can get the answer for yourself". I did remember the answer to this question, so I said, "Always line my life up with the word". He said, "Ok I got homework for you, you ready"? "YEP" I was hungry. He said, "Go to the end of the gospel John and read from there to Acts and write down every time you see the Holy Spirit in the bible and tell me what happened". So, I went back to my rack and all day I studied and every time I saw this the evidence was speaking in tongues. This was something I really did not believe in. I seen people do it in church but for real I thought they were just playing with God. The next day Lank and I met in the gym. Soon as seen him I tossed him

3 papers filled front in back with nothing but scriptures on top of scriptures. He looked at it and said "Dang lil bro you like a scribe". Then he looked at me completely disregarding the papers in his hands and said, "so what happened"? I said, "They spoke in tongues" He said, "Did you do that"? I said "NO". He looked at me and said, "Do you want what they got or the watered-down version"? It took me seconds to respond, "what they got". Then he asked me "do you believe you can do it"? My response was "I believe God can give it to me". He said, "God has already given it to you". I looked at Lank and said, "there you go talking crazy again". He starts cracking up and begins to tell me that I can do it right now. I was blown away. How could he have more confidence in me doing something than I did?

I was praying for the baptism of the Holy Ghost and the evidence of speaking in tongues for at least a month after the conversation I had with Lank. He would tell me "There is only so far we can go until you receive this thing". I ain't going to lie every time he would say that I would get offended.

April 10 is just like any other day at least that is what I thought. Lank and I were walking around the baseball field in the back of the prison by the meat plant. Shooting our regular talking about the things of God. He really had me dissecting this book week in and week out by A.W. Tozer called "The Pursuit of God". As we were walking the discussion came up again about the Holy Ghost. Lank said "Man we can only go so far in the Lord without you receiving the baptism of the Holy Ghost". Here he goes again with this Holy Ghost business quickly I am offended. "So, what you want to do? You want to pray about it?" He said in his Lanky Lank way "man you ain't trying to kick it". I shoot back "Let's go". So, we come in agreement right there on the baseball field. Lank starts praying "Lord loosen his lips in the name of Jesus". I begin to repeat what he is praying. With my eyes closed I am feeling stupid as I hear Lank speak in a language that sounds like Hebrew. I am still repeating the prayer "Lord loosen my lips". I hear Lank say "They are already loosened, speak lil bra". Now in my head I am thinking "I don't know what he expects to happen here but I aint bout to fake the funk". I can hear Lank speaking over my thoughts "speak lil bra". Suddenly I open my mouth and this utterance comes out. It did not even feel like I had enough saliva to formulate a noise let alone a word. That was all it took just that little bit of saliva and God took that, and it was over. I truly felt like I ascended above my body and was watching myself. I was aware there were people around me, but I did not care how foolish I looked, nor did I have the immediate control to stop myself. It truly was amazing I felt so safe and so loved like I was wrapped in the hands of the most loving Father. It felt like this went on for hours. It was almost like I had to fight to get back in my head to tell myself to stop speaking this language I never heard myself speak before. When I did come back, I took the biggest gasp of air and started laughing with this feeling of overwhelming joy that seemed to spread across my face into a permanent smile. I looked up at Lank and he looked back at me, and he said, "That's pretty good lil bra".

Chapter 14

Baptism by Fire

"As long as this is something my children don't believe they will receive, they won't". This is what the Lord told me regarding receiving the baptism of the Holy Ghost. I was standing believing with someone for it and He spoke this directly to my spirit. Let me clear something up right away: being born again and receiving the baptism of the Holy Spirit are two separate things.

Jesus was crucified took the curse on His physical body went through hell literally was reborn again Hebrews 1:1-5 verse 5 says "For unto which of the angels said he at any time Thou art me son this day I begotten (reborn in the Greek) thee? And again, I will be to him a father and he shall be to me a son? Jesus was the first reborn man unto God. He took the curse on his physical body Galatians 3:13 and not only physically died but spiritually died on that cross. He was separated from God, a feeling He never knew before Matthew 27:45-50. He literally went to hell as a man and suffered the penalty for every sin known to mankind Psalm 22 speaks about the horror he endured in hell. That is why we can receive the new birth because Jesus was reborn in hell and triumphed over the devil and his demons Colossians 2:14-15. He took the authority away from the devil and gave it back to the children of God Revelation 1:18. All this is possible by making Jesus the Lord of your life admitting you are a sinner and accepting Him into your heart by the words of your mouth through Faith.

Jesus rose from the grave with all power and visited Mary then He showed Himself to the disciples except Thomas. John 20: 21-22 "Then said Jesus to them again, Peace unto you: as my Father hath sent me, even so send I you". Verse 22 "And when he had said this, he breathed on them and saith unto them, receive ye the Holy Ghost:" 1 Corinthians 5:17 the Apostle Paul says, "Therefore if any man be in Christ, he is a new creature: old things are passed away: behold, all things are to become new." The moment you accepted Jesus as your savior by faith you were given a brand-new spirit. Your old sinful nature was taken away and you were given a new nature in Christ Ephesians 4:24. The Holy Spirit then came into your spirit to be a guide and teach you all things John 16:13. When you begin to renew your mind to the word of God you begin to change from the inside out Ephesians 4:23.

The baptism of the Holy spirit is when you are physically submerged in the Holy Spirit and the manifestation comes out of your mouth. In Acts 1:4 Jesus told the disciples not to depart from Jerusalem, "but wait for the promise of the Father, which ye have heard of me". Verse 5 says "For John truly baptized with water; but ye shall be baptized with the Holy Ghost not many days hence" Matthew 3:11. The day of Pentecost, Acts 2:4 "And they were all filled with the Holy Ghost, and began to speak with other tongues, as the Spirit gave utterance". The baptism Jesus was saying He would baptize them in was the baptism of the Holy Ghost and the evidence is speaking in an unknown language (tongues). What is this unknown language? Acts 2:5 reads "And there were dwelling at Jerusalem Jews devout men, out of every nation under heaven". Verse 6 "Now when this was noise abroad, the multitude came together, and were confounded, because that every man heard them speak in his own language". This proves that speaking in tongues is not just gibberish it is an actual language that is or was in the earth. Verse 10-12 tells you the languages that were being spoken people were hearing in their native tongue. "We do hear them speak in our tongues and declare the wonderful works of God".

There were two reactions of the people witnessing this event. One reaction is they were amazed and perplexed "saying one to another, what meaneth this?" The other reaction they were mocking saying "These Men are drunk." 1 Corinthians 2:4 speaks about the carnal mind meaning natural. This person only deals in the realm of the five senses. The things that are spiritual are foolish to this person's mind because they are spiritually discerned. This is how I viewed tongues when I saw it but once I found out it was God's will for not only me to receive but all of God's children, I began to believe in it. Paul certainly thought it a necessity for the disciples to receive in Acts 19:2 "Have ye received the Holy Ghost since ye believed"? Their response was "we have not so much heard whether there be any Holy Ghost." Paul then asks, "unto what then were you baptized?" "Unto John's baptism". Paul explained in verse 4 John baptized unto repentance preparing the way for Jesus and the baptism with the Holy Spirit and fire Luke 3:16. In verse 5 Paul wrote "And when they heard, they were baptized in the name of the Lord Jesus". In verse 6 "Paul laid hands on them the Holy Ghost came on them and they spake with tongues and prophesied". In the next verse it says they all spoke with tongues.

For all of those who believe this is a gift that God gives to whom he chooses and not everyone receives. I pray this will encourage you to go back and study the word accurately in context. The bible says in Romans 2:11 that God is no respect of persons. Meaning what He will do for one He will do for all that believe. In 1 Corinthians 14:2 Paul says, "for he that speaketh in an unknown tongue not unto men, but unto God: for no man understandeth him: howbeit in the spirit he speaks mysteries". That word mysteries in the Greek means a hidden or secret thing, not obvious to the understanding. In verse 4 Paul says speaking in tongues edifieth himself that word edifieth in the Greek means to build up to grow in wisdom. Now this begs the question if God is no favor of person, but he gives this gift to whom he wishes then how can he be no favor of persons? Sure, enough it sounds like some favoritism to me. The answer is he gives this gift to those that ask Luke 11:13 and believe they receive Mark 11:24. Speaking in a prayer language (tongues) unlocks the supernatural in your life. No wonder the enemy has tried so hard to keep you from it. When you speak in tongues you are using your most holy faith Jude 1:20 and according to Hebrews 11:6 it is impossible to please God without faith. If you are using your most holy faith, then I would say God is pleased. If it takes faith to please Him I do not believe using your most holy faith speaking in tongues would be something He would be holding back from any of His born-again children. Paul also said we should pray for interpretation 1 Corinthians 14:13. Not that prophesying is better than tongues. No, that is once again another lie from religion operating under the authority of Satan and his demons.

Paul said in 1 Corinthians 14:27 "If any man speaks in an unknown tongue, let it be by two, or at the most three, that by course; in the Greek means in order, and let one interpret". Paul wrote to the church in Corinth telling them if individuals are praying in tongues let it be done in order 1 Corinthians 14:33 "for God is not the author of confusion".

Now for those of you who have been church hurt. Left the altar time and time again feeling like you were not good enough and had some more repenting to do or it just wasn't meant for you to have. All of these are lies from the devil. I heard Creflo Dollar say this "for those of you who don't believe that God will fill you with His spirit because you are a dirty vessel, what other vessel does He have to fill up?" You being dirty is a prime reason why you need to be filled up. You are meant to receive this gift, but you were not meant to tarry for it. Religion has once again taught you to work for what God freely gives. This is a gift you believe by faith assurance built up in the word and continue to speak it out of your mouth. If you do not receive right away, keep standing in faith according to Ephesians 6:13. Every word of God is a seed and your coming into agreement with it out of your mouth by faith is the water that will bring the fruition.

I am going to take this time to stand in agreement with you for two things. If you are reading this book and have not been born again and are convinced of what you have read, I would like to pray you into The Kingdom right now. Repeat this prayer after me.

Heavenly Father, in the Name of Jesus, I present myself to

you. I admit that I am a sinner and I turn from my ways. I pray and ask Jesus to be Lord over my life. I believe it in my heart, so I say with my mouth that Jesus has been raised from the dead. This moment I make Him LORD over my life. Jesus, come into my heart. I believe at this moment that I am saved. I say it now. I am a Christian. I am a child of Almighty God!

The moment you prayed this prayer I believe you are a new creation in Christ Jesus; old things have passed away; behold all things have become new according to 2 Corinthians 5:17-21. I believe this transformation has taken place right now. You have been translated out of the kingdom of darkness into the kingdom of His dear Son according to Colossians 1:13. The Blessing is available to you. I would encourage you to get to a church that preaches and teaches on the kingdom and how to operate in it. Remember in the Greek Gospel means Good News so if what you are hearing is not good news it probably is not the Gospel. No matter how much the devil tries to disguise it.

Prayer for the Baptism of the Holy Ghost and the evidence of speaking in tongues.

Father You said in your word ask and it will be given to me; seek and I will find; knock and the door will be opened; Well Father I am asking; I am seeking and I am knocking at the door to be

filled with the Holy Spirit and the evidence of
speaking in tongues as the spirit gives
utterance. I believe this is a good gift that you
desire to give to your children. I declare I am
your child, and you are a good Father. I receive
the baptism of the Holy Ghost in the name of
Jesus Christ. I thank you for it and I have it Now!
Now open your mouth and start speaking in a language
other than your native one and start praising Him
Hallelujah!

You cannot receive this with your mind, it must be
received in the heart. Study the scriptures that pertain to
this subject. Stand on the word, declare it out your
mouth and praise Him daily and you will experience this
amazing gift in the name of Jesus.

Chapter 15

The Old Man Dies

After being baptized in fire and speaking in tongues that is when I was opened up to the supernatural. The bible says to meditate in the word day and night Psalm 1:2 and that is exactly what I did. I stayed in the word so much God was showing me visions and even reading me scriptures when I slept. I actually rewrote the entire New Testament.

One of the most intense experiences that I had was in the church. My favorite part of the services in prison was praise and worship. When the music would start, I would close my eyes, begin to pray in the spirit and be taken away almost like i was touching heaven. Lank was the head of the praise team and I'm telling you what a man could get his breakthrough in that environment. There I was praying in the spirit listening to the sound of the instruments. I could feel the Holy Spirit all over me. I began to tell God "I want to feel your power." Right as I said this, I could feel something inside of me shaking. I said it again this time directing the Holy Spirit where I wanted to feel it "I want to feel it in my legs." The moment these words were released out of my mouth my legs started shaking. The music was still playing in the background, and everyone was standing up. With my eyes fluttering I could feel tears running down my cheeks. They were not tears of sadness but tears of Joy. At this point my entire body is shaking with every command I give "Let me feel it in my arms, in my chest, in my head." His presence and power was surging through my entire body. I had no control at this point but even if I could have stopped, I did not want to. It was as if my mind was one with God and He was allowing me to feel Him. At this point all music stopped and there I am standing up in the entire church having this episode. I could feel someone's hand on my back. I could not speak but I did not want him to touch me. I knew I was safe. I just had this assurance that nothing could harm me absolutely nothing. I could hear very faintly "don't touch him he is fine if you have never trusted anything in all your life trust me, He is in good hands "I later found out the voice I heard was from the Chaplain. When I did snap out of it everything around me was moving so slow. I stumbled out of the building and made it to the water fountain I could barely drink. The CO looked at me and said, "Are you ok?" I still could not talk. I was very weak, and I felt physically drained. The best way to explain that feeling was like a volcano was in my body and I felt like I was going to explode but I knew I was safe I knew nothing could hurt me.

I eventually went back in to hear the word, but I could not concentrate. What just happened was so supernatural I could not think about anything else. When service let out, I heard people laughing on the way to the dorm. "Bro was in there faking the Holy Spirit'. I did not care; I knew what I experienced was legit. Then an older white man came up to me and told me, "Thank You. I have never seen anything like that in my entire life. Thank you". I told him "It wasn't me it was all God". I went back to my dorm laid down on my rack and praised God until they called chow.

After chow, a guy I knew that used to be Pastor on the streets at one time came up to me and said these exact words "God was depositing something in you whatever it is, it's powerful and whatever it is you're going to need it".

The crazy thing is every time I would see the guy that was sitting next to me that day. He would look at me in the strangest way like he had no idea what he was looking at like I was an alien. I finally decided to speak to him one day walking to school. I went up to him and said, "You were holding me up that day in church, weren't you?" He looked at me in this very strange way and said "yes" very quietly. I then asked him "what did it feel like when you were holding me?" He looked at me and said, "Like electricity was going through your body". Then he turned around and walked off. I turned around and started walking the opposite direction and then turned back around and I saw him looking directly at me with that strange look on his face. He then turned back around and walked off. This was the last time I saw him.

I ended up doing a little over six years in prison. Those last two years changed my life. I praise God for my sister's adopted mom, Lisi, she always came to see me and spoke life. "Kirk be like Joseph, be different from all the other inmates, rise to the top by being respectful and doing what you are told". Well, I did. I went from having the worst job and the worst reputation to the best job and apologizing to CO's when I was in the wrong. I truly had favor even down to my last day. I remember the guy from the halfway house came to pick me up and it was around count time he looked at me and said, "They usually don't let people out around this time". I looked back at him and said, "Yeah, I like to believe I got favor ". He said, "Yes I agree in all my years of picking people up from prison I have never heard the CO's say anything good but when I mentioned your name the guy at the desk said, "Oh Kirk yea he won't be back". He was wrong.

I have gone back in many different institutions including P.C.I. as well as juvenile facilities telling my story. I am know longer a plague to my community but a changing agent all by the grace of God. The old man is dead and buried. I truly understand what Lank was telling me that day when He asked me if I believe I am a new creation in Christ Jesus? I am, I am everything God's word says I am, and because I believe that my life is a reflection of my new life in Christ. The old man died on that road to Damascus.

The thing that is different about my story is I did not cry out to God. He supernaturally came into my life, and it changed me forever. I could have been content living the rest of my life distant from him because for me ignorance was bliss. So, I wake up every day and praise Him and thank God that I do not have to.

I still use my gift of writing, but I use it for spoken word. I know longer write about the struggle, hustling and the storms of life. I use my gift to glorify the Lord and how we are more than conquerors in Christ Jesus. By the grace of God, I have been able to perform on many platforms in Columbus Ohio. As long as I am on this earth, I will continue giving my gift to the world.

If you know someone who is behind bars, never give up on them. I know it was the effectual prayers of the righteous that had a lot to do with my transformation. God loves the prisoner, and he still sets the captives free today Spirit Soul and Body.

THIS IS TRULY JUST THE BEGINNING!